Mythical Beast Investigator

BERNARD'S RAGE AT LOSING WHAT MATTERED MOST TO HIM IN THE WORLD COULD ONLY BE QUENCHED BY HIM CARRYING OUT HIS MISSION.
HE YEARNED FOR REVENGE AND WOULD NEVER FORGIVE ANYONE WHO PREVENTED HIM FROM TAKING IT.
EACH-UISGE...

HE'S DEADLY SERIOUS ABOUT THIS.
IF I INTERVENE UNNECES-SARILY...
HE MAY CARRY THIS GUILT FOR THE REST OF HIS LIFE.
BWUP

SPLASH
SPLASH
ぱしゃ...
SPLASH SPLASH SPLASH
ぱしゃぱしゃぱしゃ
SPLASH SPLASH SPLASH
ぱしゃ ぱしゃぱしゃ
IT'S HERE!!
SURGE
KUSHUNA.
PLEASE STEP IN IF HIS LIFE IS IN DANGER.
AS YOU WISH.
SPLASH
ぱしゃ
SPLASH
ぱしゃ
SPLASH
ぱしゃ
GWOOOOOH
SPLISH

GALLOP

GALLOP
GWOOOOOH
FWUP
GALLOP

YAAAAAAHHHH!!
TUNK
SLIIIISSSH

NEERAAA
SPLURT
FWUP
FWUP
FWUP
FWUP

SPLOSH
SPLOSH
DID I GET IT?!
IT WASN'T FATAL!
HE'LL ATTACK AGAIN!!
ZWOOOM

BWAM
CRACK
CRACK
SPLAAASH
ZA-PLASH
NGH...
KOFF!
GAH!
SPA-
LOOSH
UNH......!!
SPLISSSH

NREEE!!
FWOO
SWOOP
KU-
SHUNA
!!

OOOWOOOOOO!!
OOOOOOOOH!!!!
GRIM ...!
HE CRIED OUT!

GNARSH
THRASH
THRASH
BWOOM
BWOOM
CLENCH
GNAW
GNAW

NREEEEEEEE-!
DASH
SPLOSH
LURCH
GRIM...!
LURCH
NGH!
URK!
SPLASH
BERNARD!
SLOSH
SLOSH

I-I'LL BE FINE.
NGH...
BUT... SOME BONES ARE BROKEN. I CAN'T MOVE...
PLEASE...
PLEASE GO TO HIM!
SLOOSH

SLOOSH
SLOOSH
squirm
もぞ
squirm
もぞ
TROW?
FLAP
FLAP
SLOOSH
WOBBLE
......
RRRRIP
ビッ
UGH! SO SLOW!

AH!
ZA-PLASH
THIS WILL BE FAR FASTER!
KUSHUNA?
A LADY LIKE YOURSELF SHOULD NOT REND YOUR CLOTHING, MY FLOWER!
PLEASE FIND HIM, KUSHUNA!

KUSHUNA!
I SEE.

FWSH
FWSSSSH
SPLOSH
THROB
THROB...

"THIS POWERLESSNESS AND ANGER I FEEL WON'T BE BANISHED IF I LEAVE IT TO SOMEONE ELSE."
"WHEN OUR VILLAGE SET ASIDE A NEW GRAVEYARD, HE WAS DUE TO BE BURIED ALIVE THERE AS ITS GUARDIAN DOG-SPIRIT. MY DAUGHTER INTERVENED AND SAVED HIM."
"MY SOUL WILL GUARD THE GRAVEYARD AFTER I DIE!"
YOU HATED THAT CREATURE ...
JUST AS MUCH, DIDN'T YOU?

SHLOP
Stagger
FWUMP
HIS WOUNDS ARE BAD.
HE'S...
Drip
Drip
Drip

Plip
ポ
Plip
ポ
Plip
ポ
ZHP
SPLASH

HIS CONSCIOUSNESS IS FADING.
NUZZLE
sniff sniff
RUB
IT WOULD APPEAR HE HAS MISTAKEN YOU FOR SOMEONE ELSE, MY FLOWER.
HE IS ACTING LIKE A SMALL PUP WHO WISHES TO BE SPOILED BY HIS MASTER.

HWOOO...
FWMP...

CLOSE
THIS STRIKES YOU AS UNUSUAL BEHAVIOR FOR ME?
I SUPPOSE SO.
SHWP

IT SEEMS ONLY RIGHT TO OFFER MY RESPECTS, FROM ONE LOYAL SERVANT TO ANOTHER.
WE MUST TELL BERNARD.
THIS CHILD SHOULD BE BURIED IN THE CEMETERY HIS MISTRESS NOW GUARDS.
MY FLOWER.
DO YOU BELIEVE THE GRAVEYARD GUARDIAN AND THIS ELDERLY DOG WILL MEET ONCE AGAIN?
I COULDN'T SAY.
THERE'S NO KNOWING WHERE HER SOUL HAS TRULY GONE.
HOWEVER...

I DO BELIEVE THAT NOW THEY'RE BOTH FREE TO GO WHEREVER THEY WISH.

Mythical Beast Investigator

妖精猫の猫裁判

Trial of the Cat Sith

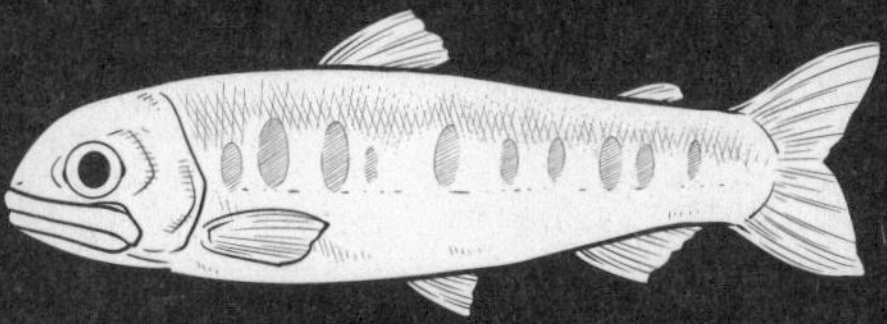

[Chapter 7]

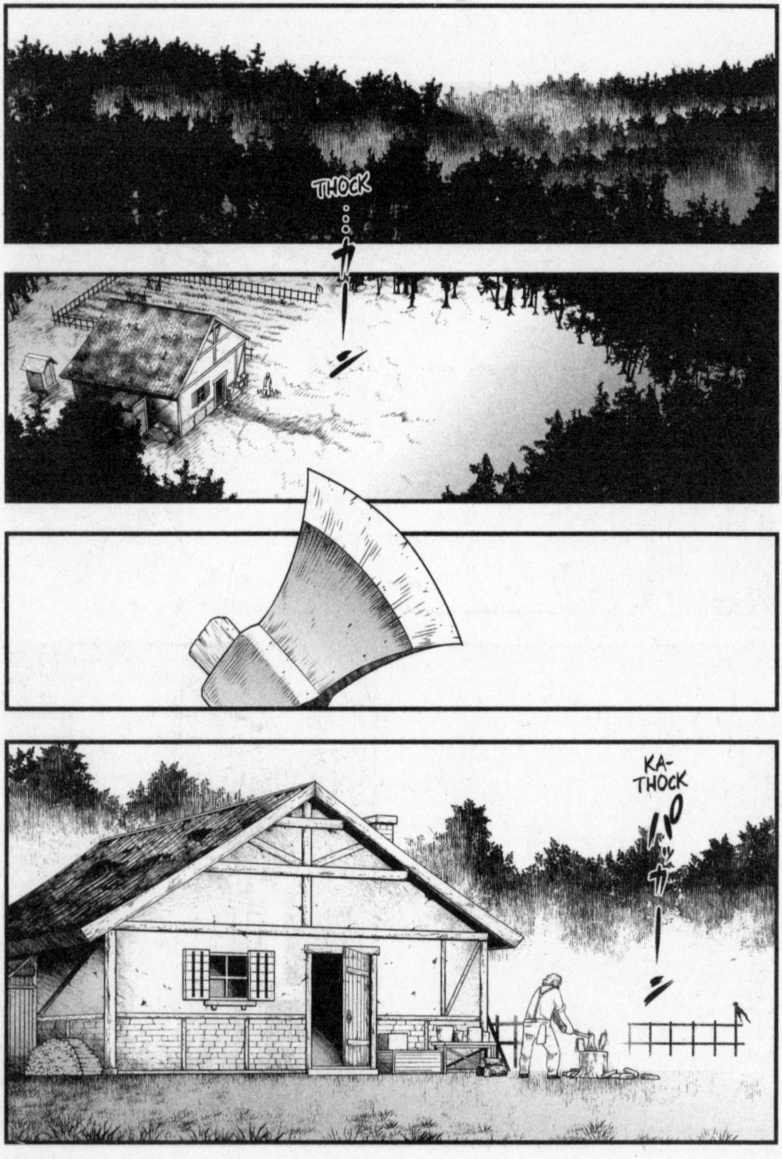
THOCK
……カーン
KA-THOCK
パッカーン

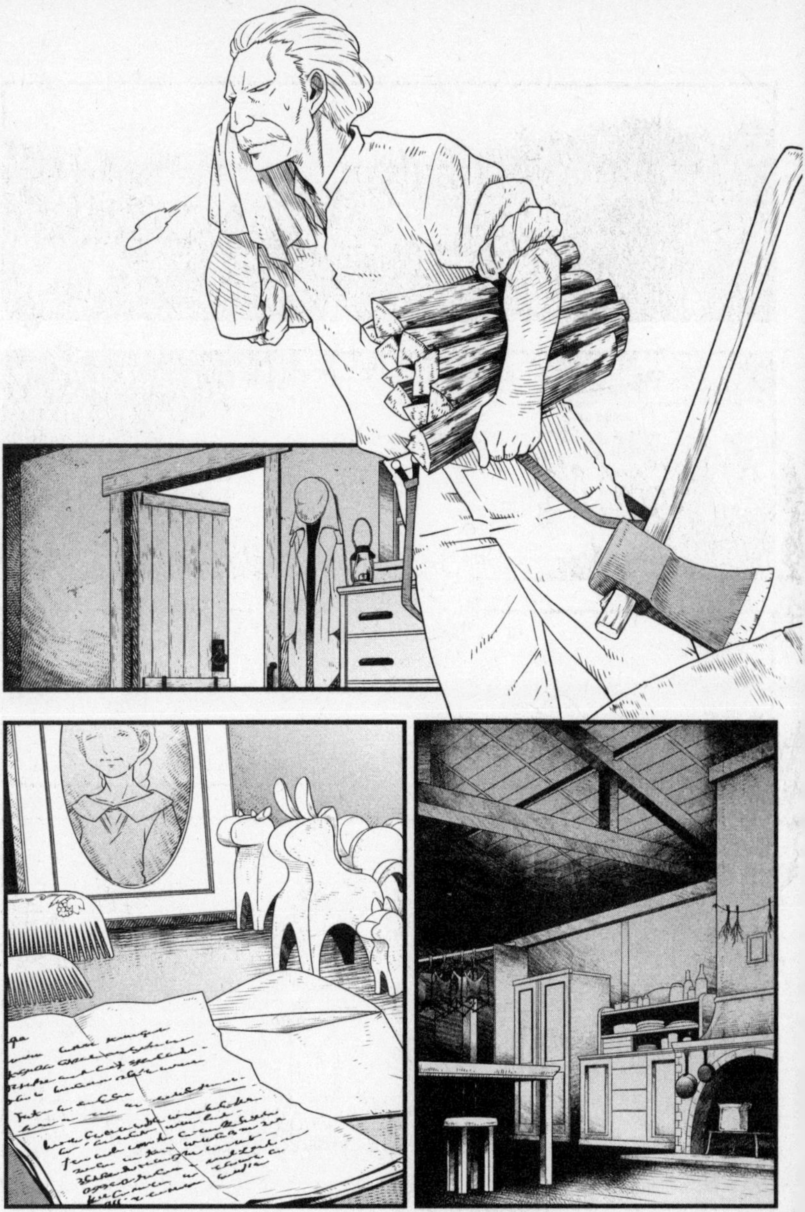

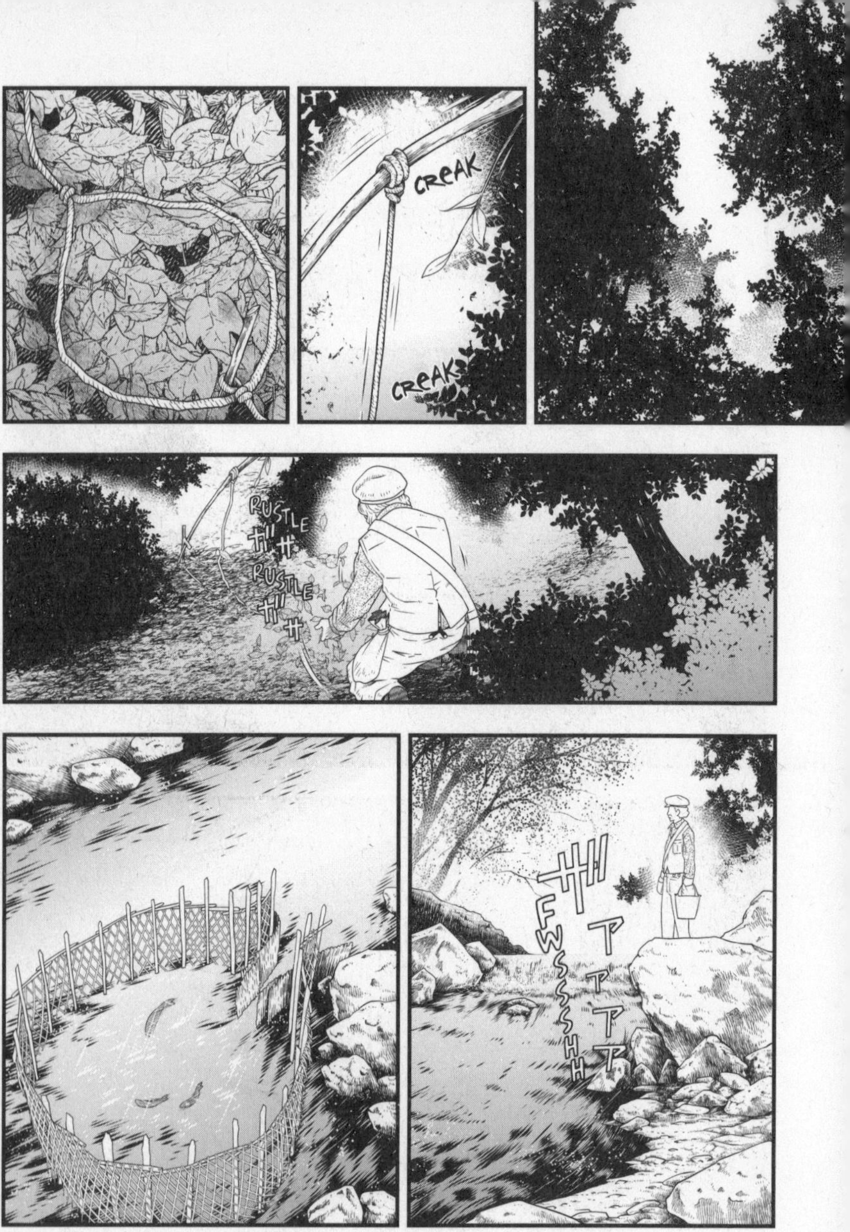
CREAK
CREAK
RUSTLE
RUSTLE
FWSSSHH

SPLISH
SPLASH
SPLISH
TMP
TMP
SPLISH

CHIRP CHIRP CHIRP...
HMM.
THE FISH I SAVED FOR LATER IS GONE AGAIN TODAY.
HOW MANY TIMES DOES THAT MAKE IT?
I WOULDN'T MIND IF IT WERE MY DEAD WIFE'S GHOST SNEAKING IN AT NIGHT TO EAT IT, BUT...
SHE NEVER LIKED FRESHWATER FISH.
......

RUSTLE
RUSTLE
RUSTLE
RUSTLE
I'M SCARED OF GHOSTS, BUT...
I'D STILL LIKE TO SEE ONE.
I ALMOST FEEL LIKE I'M A KID AGAIN.
NOD
NOD

CREEEAK...
TONK
HOOK
SPLASH

YOU...
GRRR!
LITTLE ...!
GRAB
NYAAOOOO!!!!
SLIP
WHAM
BONK
FWIP
SCURRY
SCURRY
SCURRY

......
......
FLOP FLOP
SPLISH
WHEW...
TRUDGE
もそ
TRUDGE
もそ

......
"DEAR...
"DEAR, YOU SHOULDN'T PULL A CAT'S TAIL LIKE THAT!"
I'M SORRY, HONEY.
I DIDN'T THINK IT WOULD HURT IT THAT MUCH.
SHOULD I PUT THE BUCKET OUTSIDE FOR THE CAT AS AN APOLOGY?
NO.
AFTER I TREATED IT LIKE THAT...
I DOUBT IT'LL EVER COME HERE AGAIN.
CREAK

JOLT
ガバッ
ぞろ TP
ぞろ TP

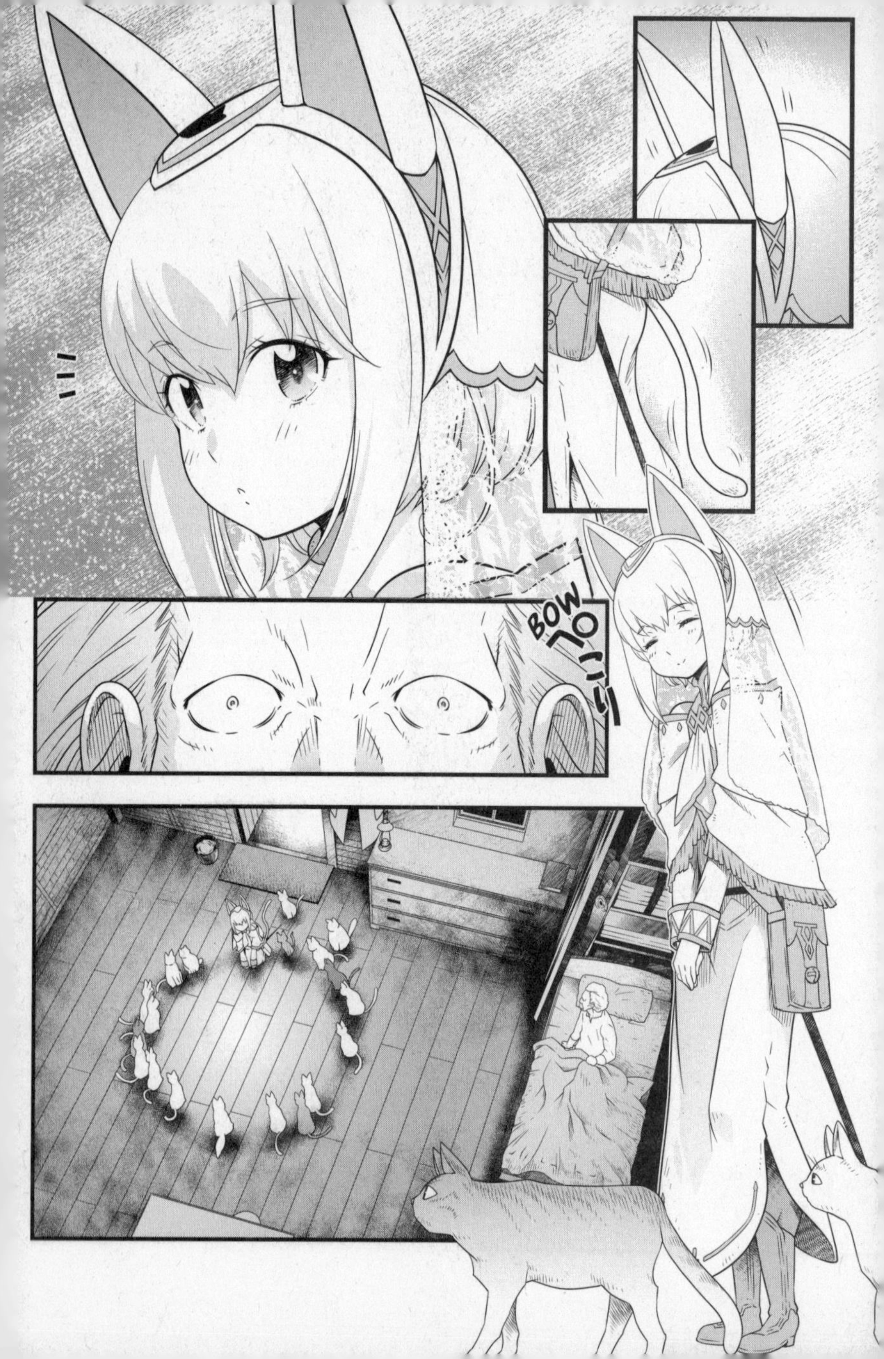
BOW

MRROW!
なあご
MRROW!
なあご
MRROW!
なあご
MRROW!
なあご
MRROW!
なあご
CREAK...
CREAK...
CREAK...
MRROW!
なあご
MRROW!
なあご
MRROW!
なあご
CREAK...

MEOW! MEOW! MEOW!
MEOW! NYAAAA!
TMP
TMP
TMP...
FWUP
プラーン
DANGLE
BWOOM
BWOOM
STMP
STMP
THUD
MRRAH!—
バターン
FLOP...
SHAKE
SHAKE

?!!
SHWP
......

UNI! UNINI!
UMI!
UNYAA!
?!
?!
UNI!
MUNCH はむ
MUNCH はむ
SWIP
SHAKe
SHAKe
UMYA!
MRRYA! NYAMU!
KANAAH!
NYA NYA NYA NYA!
NYAGOU!

NYAA!
NYAA!
NYAMU!
NYA!
NYAA!
SPIN
SHTP
ZWOOOOSH
NYAGO!
FLINCH

THMP
THMP
SILENCE...

SHUP
のし
SHF
FWAP
ぱかん
CHOMP
MEW...
TMP
スタ
TMP
スタ

DAZED
THANK YOU FOR ALLOWING ME TO TAKE PART!
WHAT A PRIVILEGE TO WITNESS A CAT SITH TRIAL!
OH.
PAUSE

YOU WERE FOUND INNOCENT.
CON-GRATULA-TIONS.
......
KA-CHAK
WHAT IN THE WORLD JUST HAPPENED ...?

SIZZ ジ
SIZZ ジ
TOK

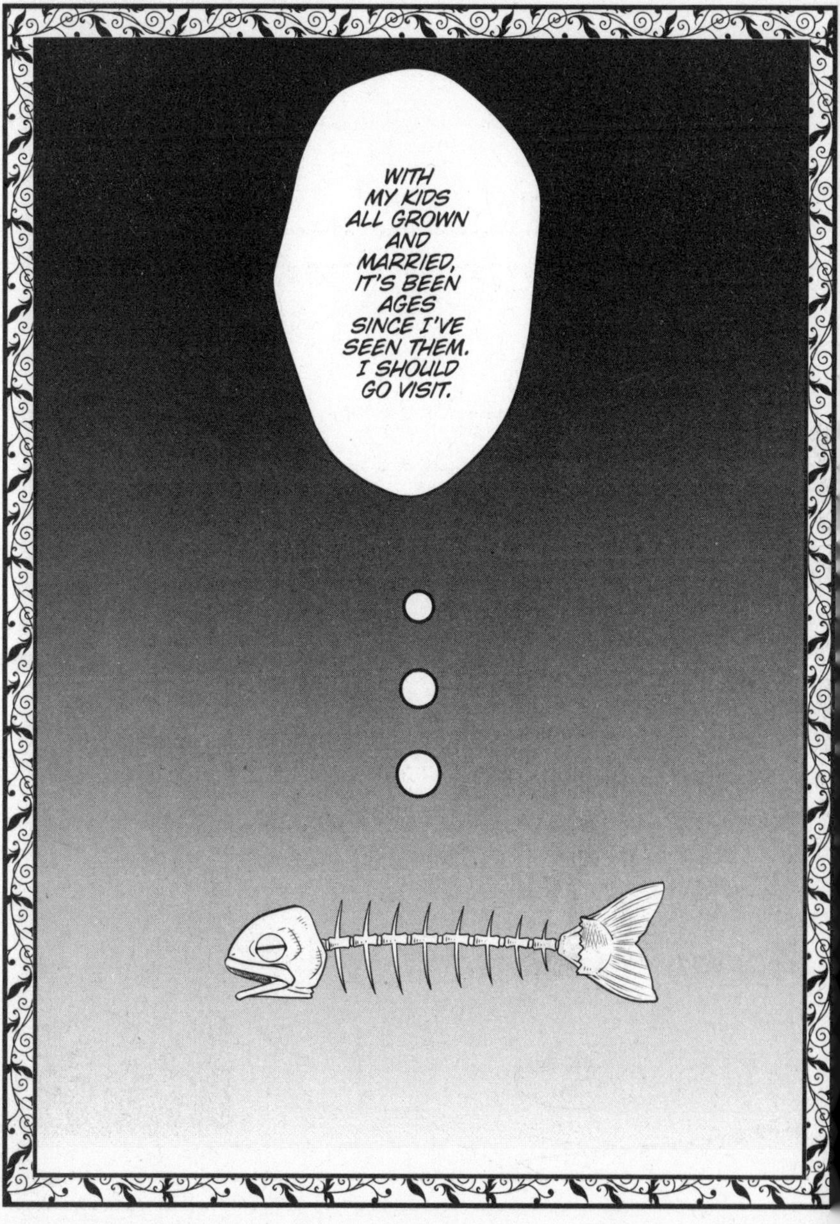
WITH MY KIDS ALL GROWN AND MARRIED, IT'S BEEN AGES SINCE I'VE SEEN THEM. I SHOULD GO VISIT.

Mythical Beast Investigator

[Chapter 8]
The Tale of the King of Darkness

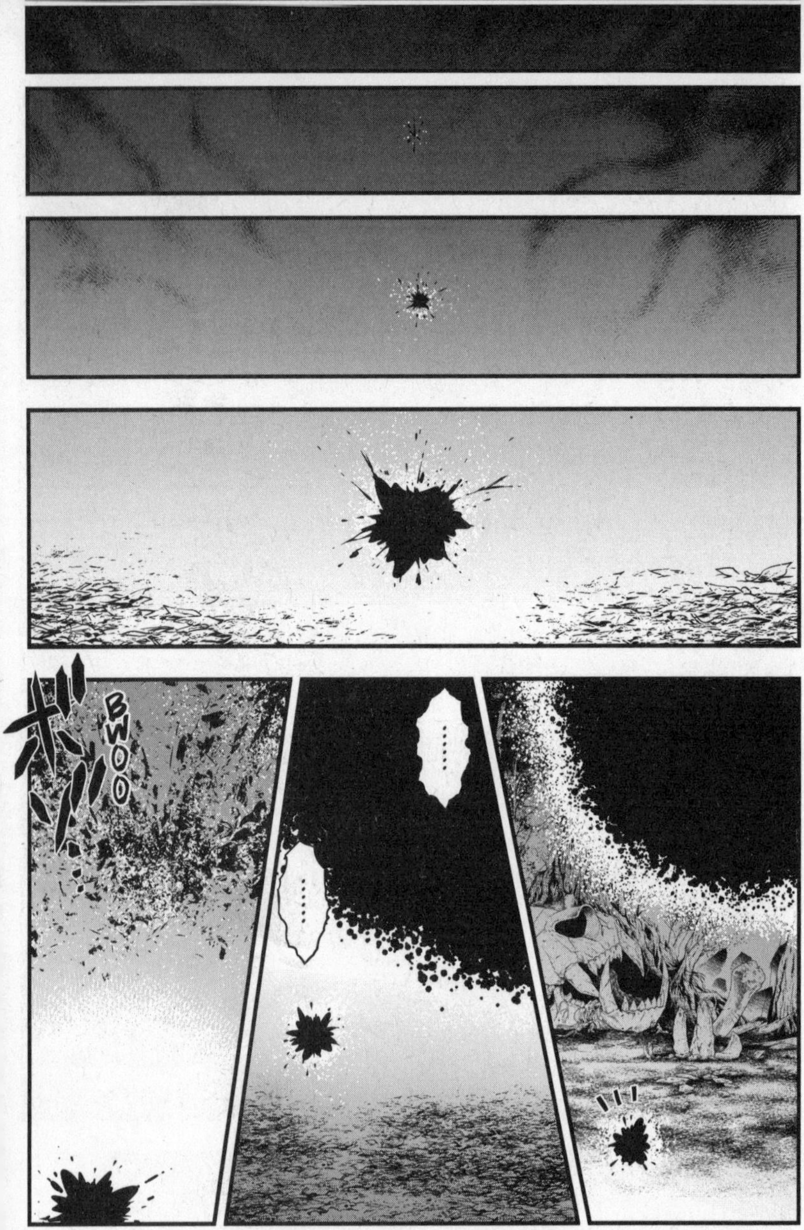
BWOO
……
……

RUSTLE
TWITCH
HOP
GHH
GH
GH
GH
GH...

FWOOOOOOH!
RAAAAH

SWHP
?!!
ZUU
わあああ あぁ
GYAAAAAH!
Zuu
Zuu
Zuu
Zuu
Zuu

SNAP
ZUU
ZUU
ZUU
ZUU
ZUU
ZUU...

RUSTLE
RUSTLE
RUSTL
RUSTLE
RUSTLE
ZUU
ZUU
ZUU
ZUU
ZUU
ZUU

THIS STRETCH OF TIME WAS LONG AND TEDIOUS, BUT IT ALSO PASSED QUICKLY.
CLENCH
SHWOO
SHWOO

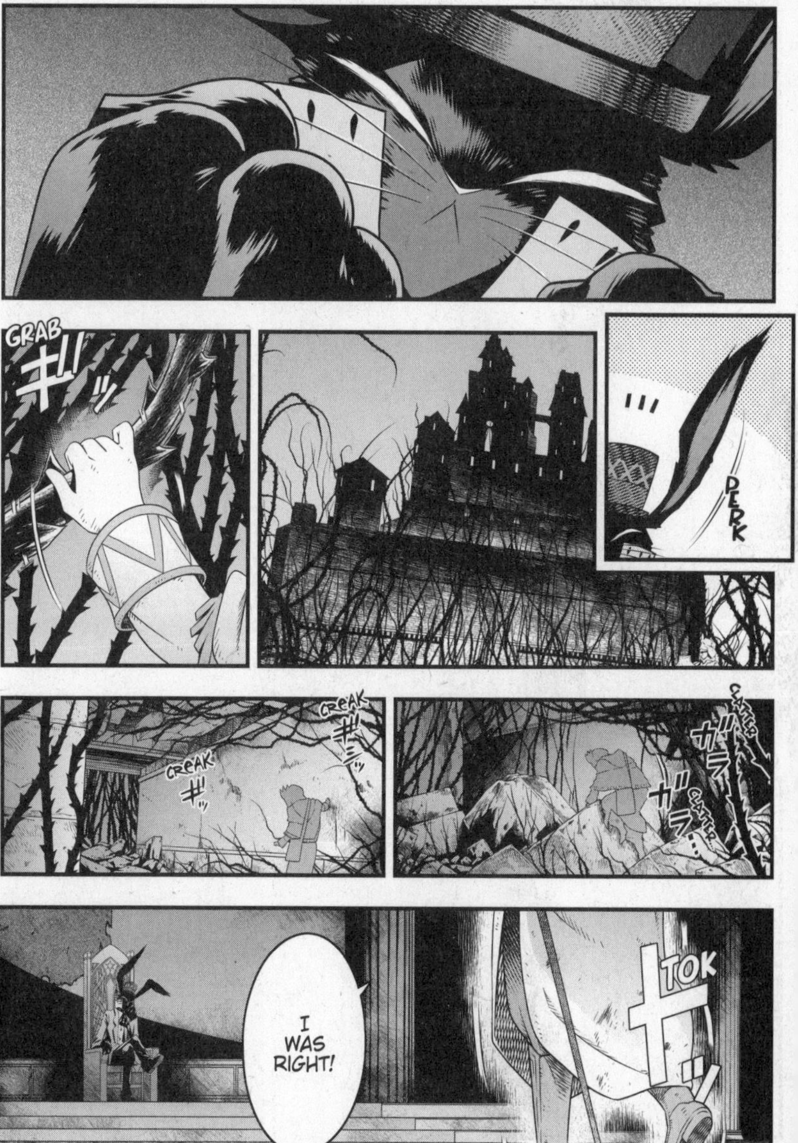
PERK
GRAB
CLATTER
CLATTER...
CREAK
CREAK
TOK
I WAS RIGHT!

THE "DEMON KING" SAID TO LIVE IN THIS CASTLE IS A MYTHICAL BEAST!
IT'S A PLEA-SURE TO MEET YOU!
I AM A MYTHICAL BEAST INVESTIGATOR, TASKED WITH RECORDING INFORMATION ABOUT MYTHICAL BEASTS. ONCE IT'S IN THIS BOOK, THAT KNOWLEDGE CAN BE SHARED FAR AND WIDE!
IN MY TRAVELS, I SEARCH FOR WAYS FOR HUMANS AND MYTHICAL BEASTS TO LIVE TOGETHER IN HARMONY.
AND YOU SEEM TO BE AN UNRECORDED TYPE OF MYTHICAL BEAST.
......
SNAP

......
FLING
ZUU
ZUU
ZUU
ZUU
PLEASE, WOULD YOU HEAR ME OUT?
YOU SURPRISED ME!
ACTUALLY, THE MORE I LOOK AT YOU...
THE MORE LIKELY IT SEEMS THAT...
YOU SPRING FROM BOTH MYTHICAL BEASTS AND SOME TYPE OF *SPIRIT*--ALTHOUGH HUMANITY CURRENTLY HAS ONLY **THEORIES** ABOUT THE EXISTENCE OF SPIRITS.

I CAN'T BELIEVE TWO SUCH DIFFERENT SPECIES COMINGLED!
PERHAPS THERE WAS SOME SPECIAL REASON FOR IT...?
YOUR VERY EXISTENCE IS A RARITY, AND YOU'RE QUITE POWERFUL...
WOULD YOU PLEASE SPEAK WITH ME?
SNAP
FLING
ZUUU
ZUUU
ZUUU
ZUUU
......

I UNDER-STAND.
I'LL ASK QUESTIONS LATER.
TATTERED
FOR NOW, WOULD YOU PLEASE ALLOW ME TO SKETCH YOU?
......

ZWIP
SCAMPER
SCAMPER
SCAMPER
I'LL FIND A CORNER TO SLEEP IN.
JUST PRETEND I'M NOT HERE.

JUST BECAUSE YOU'RE BORED, THAT DOESN'T MEAN YOU SHOULD DO BAD THINGS!

YOU'RE CAPABLE OF SINGLEHANDEDLY THROWING THE ECOSYSTEM AS WE KNOW IT INTO CHAOS.
FOR ALL I KNOW, THAT MAY HAVE BEEN THE ORIGINAL PURPOSE BEHIND YOUR CREATION.
BUT YOU MUSTN'T HURT PEOPLE OR BEASTS. THE ONLY RESULT OF THAT WOULD BE SORROW.
AND YET...
AS A CREATURE WHO EXISTS FOR THAT VERY PURPOSE...
IS THAT NOT MY **DUTY?**
ALL LIVING THINGS CAN CHOOSE TO LIVE AS THEY WISH, WHETHER OR NOT IT ALIGNS WITH THEIR PARENTS' PLANS.
BESIDES, SINCE THE MOMENT YOU WERE BORN...
YOU'VE ONLY EVER WITNESSED SCENES OF GREAT SADNESS.
YOU STILL KNOW NOTHING ABOUT THE WONDERS AND JOYS OF THIS WORLD.
IF YOU DESTROY EVERYTHING AROUND YOU OUT OF BOREDOM, ONE DAY YOU'LL REGRET IT.

SILENCE, YOU INSECT!
WHAT DO YOU KNOW OF ME? SHALL I SHUT YOUR MOUTH FOR YOU?!
I WILL NOT BE SILENT!
YOU'RE THE ONE WHO SHOULD REEVALUATE YOUR WAYS.
TO BEGIN WITH, STAYING IN A LONELY PLACE LIKE THIS IS NO GOOD!
TURN
SO FIRST...

SSSNAP...
ZUU
ZUU
ZUU
HEY, YOU IRRITATING INSECT! WHAT MEANING IS THERE IN DOING SOMETHING LIKE THIS?
THERE IS NO MEANING. SO MANY WONDERFUL THINGS IN THIS WORLD ARE MEANINGLESS.
SO YOU CLAIM, BUT...
NEXT, PLEASE REMOVE THE DEBRIS FROM THE STAIRS. I'D LIKE TO PROPERLY INVESTIGATE THE LIBRARY.
......

SOME STORIES ARE ABOUT THOSE WHO FOUGHT BRAVELY FOR THEIR BRETHREN.
OTHERS ARE ABOUT PROTECTING THE WEAK.
THE EVENTS DESCRIBED IN SOME OF THESE BOOKS MUST HAVE TRULY HAPPENED.
YOU ARE NEEDLESSLY RESILIENT.
WELL, THAT'S MY BEST QUALITY, AFTER ALL.
ZZZ...
ZZZ...

"YOU MUST NOT HURT OR KILL HUMANS.
"NATURALLY, YOU MUST NOT KILL MYTHICAL BEASTS EITHER.
"YOU SHOULD NOT DESTROY BEASTS OR HUMANS JUST BECAUSE YOU'ARE BORED.
"DON'T LET YOURSELF STAY TRAPPED IN THIS BOREDOM FOREVER."
"FOOL! HOW DARE A'MERE INSECT SPEAK SO TO ME?"
"BECAUSE I DON'T WANT YOU TO WIND UP FILLED WITH REGRET."
"I SHOULD SIMPLY KILL YOU AND LEAVE YOU IN A STATE OF EVERLAST-ING PAIN."
"IF THAT'S TRULY WHAT YOU WISH TO DO, FEEL FREE. IT WON'T SHAKE MY RESOLVE."
"I'LL DO IT, I SWEAR!"

"WHEN, THEN?"
"OH, SHUT UP!"

IS THERE SOME PRICE I MUST PAY TO EARN YOUR SILENCE?!
ZU
SHFF
NO, NO.
I AM QUITE AWARE THAT HUMANS FIGHT OVER LAND AND WEALTH.
I DEMANDED YOUR SILENCE AND YET OFFERED NOTHING IN RETURN. WHAT DO YOU WISH FOR?
YOU MAY BE NOISY, BUT YOU HAVE QUELLED A BIT OF MY BOREDOM.
I SHALL GRANT YOU ANYTHING YOU WISH, WHATEVER IT MAY BE.

THERE'S NOTHING I WANT.
IS THAT SO?
IT IS.
I SEE. SO THERE IS NOTHING YOU WANT...
THERE'S NOTHING I WANT, BUT I DO HAVE A WISH. MY WISH IS FOR YOU TO NOT BRING HARM TO ANY CREATURE.
THAT IS ALL?
YES.
I SEE. THAT'S HOW IT IS.
OH, BUT...
HM?

I WAS WONDERING, DO YOU EVER INTEND TO LEAVE THIS CASTLE?
WHAT?
WHY DOES THAT CONCERN YOU?
INSTEAD OF STAYING IN SUCH A DREADFULLY LONELY PLACE...
I THINK YOU SHOULD COME WITH ME.
GRR!
GRR!
GRR!
GRR!
GRR!

WHY SHOULD I?
ESPECIALLY AT THE WHIM OF A PESKY INSECT?
KNOW YOUR PLACE!
SUCH A NOISY HUMAN...
ONCE THAT NOISY BUG DEPARTS...
I WILL ONCE AGAIN...
AHH...
THAT'S RIGHT.
THERE IS NOTHING THAT KEEPS ME HERE ALONE IN THIS CASTLE.

ALL RIGHT, THEN. REJOICE!
TA-DA!
GOOD.
I HAVE DECIDED TO ACCOMPANY YOU!
NOT MUCH OF A RE-SPONSE.

THAT MAKES ME SO HAPPY!
THANK YOU!

Mythical Beast Investigator

[Chapter 9]
Madness of an Ancient Dragon

BA-CHING
TROW?
SHAKE
SHAKE
A NOTICE FROM ANOTHER INVESTIGATOR, USING THE HOMUNCULUS'S ABILITY.
ZAA
ZAA
ZAA...
The ancient dragon has awakened.
BZZ-CHK

......
OH NO.
TROW, RELAY THAT SIGNAL AS FAR AND WIDE AS YOU CAN.

Tomorrow, an investigator from the royal capital will be deployed to join the case and begin investigating.
All investigators, stand by. Maintain your positions.
ZAA ZAA...
THAT'LL TAKE TOO LONG!
THEY WON'T MAKE IT! WHY WOULD THEY DECIDE TO DO THAT?!
OF ALL THE SPECIES OF DRAGONS, THE ANCIENT ONES ARE MOST LIKE THE DRAGONS OF OLD. ALL INFORMATION ABOUT THEM IS KEPT SECRET.
PRESUMABLY A TEAM IS BEING ASSEMBLED THAT IS BOTH SKILLED ENOUGH TO FACE THE DRAGON AND HIGH-LEVEL ENOUGH TO BE TRUSTED WITH INFORMATION ABOUT IT.
ONE MUST WONDER HOW MANY PEOPLE MEET SUCH CRITERIA, HOWEVER.
IF THE ANCIENT DRAGON CRAWLS OUT OF THE WORLD'S DEPTHS, THE SURROUNDING LAND WILL BE POISONED AND LAID WASTE! MANY PEOPLE AND CREATURES WILL DIE, AND THE ECO-SYSTEM WILL CRUMBLE!
HOW CAN THEY NOT SEE THAT IT WOULD TAKE A CENTURY TO RECOVER?!

THEY DO NOT UNDER-STAND HOW DIRE THE SITUATION IS.
I HEAR THAT THOSE WHO OUT-RANK THE INVESTIGA-TORS HAVE THEIR HEADS TOO DEEPLY LODGED IN BOOKS TO UNDERSTAND THE REAL WORLD.
WHAT IS YOUR COURSE OF ACTION? ORDINARILY, ONE WOULD AWAIT A HERO'S ARRIVAL.
I CAN'T DO THAT.
TOO MANY HUMANS AND MYTHICAL BEASTS ARE ABOUT TO DIE, AND...
THERE'S A CHANCE THAT THE INVESTIGATOR WHO SENT THE SIGNAL IS STILL ALIVE.
I'VE...
I'VE BEEN WORKING SO HARD TO PREVENT SOMETHING LIKE THIS!
RUB RUB
BUT NOW...

GWOOOOH
PLEASE ACCOMPANY ME.
AS YOU WISH.

GRWOO
FWROO
THE FISSURE IS ALREADY OPEN. HE'LL EMERGE SOON.
RUMBLE
I DO WISH YOU'D STAY BEHIND, TROW.
SHAKE
SHAKE
SHAKE
TAKE HIM ALONG.
I WOULD MAKE THE SAME CHOICE.
WHAT MEANING WOULD HE FIND IN LIVING ON ALONE?

THIS IS SO AWFUL. IT'S JUST LIKE THE LEGENDS SAY.
IN ORDER TO QUELL THE WILD MAGIC, THE CREATURE BECAME ONE WITH THE EARTH...AND LOST THE ABILITY TO DIE.
ZUU
ZUU
ZUU
THE SHEER QUANTITY OF MAGIC HE ABSORBED FROM THE VEINS OF THE WORLD OVER THE COURSE OF HIS ENDLESS LIFE...
WAS ENOUGH TO DESTROY EVEN THE WILL OF A DRAGON.
UNABLE TO DIE, THE PROUD DRAGON DESCENDED INTO MADNESS WHILE PROTECTING THE LAND, AND NO OTHER DRAGONS HAVE INTERVENED.
IT CANNOT BE HELPED.
WE MUST PUT IT OUT OF ITS MISERY BEFORE IT DESTROYS THE VERY LAND IT ONCE PROTECTED.
NO MATTER WHAT HAPPENS TO ME...
PLEASE STOP HIM.
AFTER THAT, GO WHEREVER YOU PLEASE... BUT PROMISE ME YOU'LL TAKE TROW WITH YOU.
THAT WAY NEITHER OF YOU WILL BE LONELY.
FOOL.
AS IF I WOULD PERMIT THIS CREATURE TO HARM YOU.
RUMBLE
DO NOT FRET. I'LL GIVE YOU THE DRAGON'S HEART AS A GIFT.
I'LL SERVE IT UP ON A PLATTER!
RUMBLE
ZUU ZUU

THERE WAS PAIN AND SORROW.
AGRAAAGH!
LAMENTATION. RAGE. FURY.
FEAR. DESPAIR. HORROR.
BUT ALSO... JUBILATION.

CRACK
CRACK
CRACK
GYAAAAAARRRRH!
THE ANCIENT DRAGON HAD BEEN UTTERLY CONSUMED BY MADNESS.
FWOOOOOO

GUSH
GYAAARH!
ZUU
SPLAT SPLAT SPLAT SPLAT
A SPRING!!

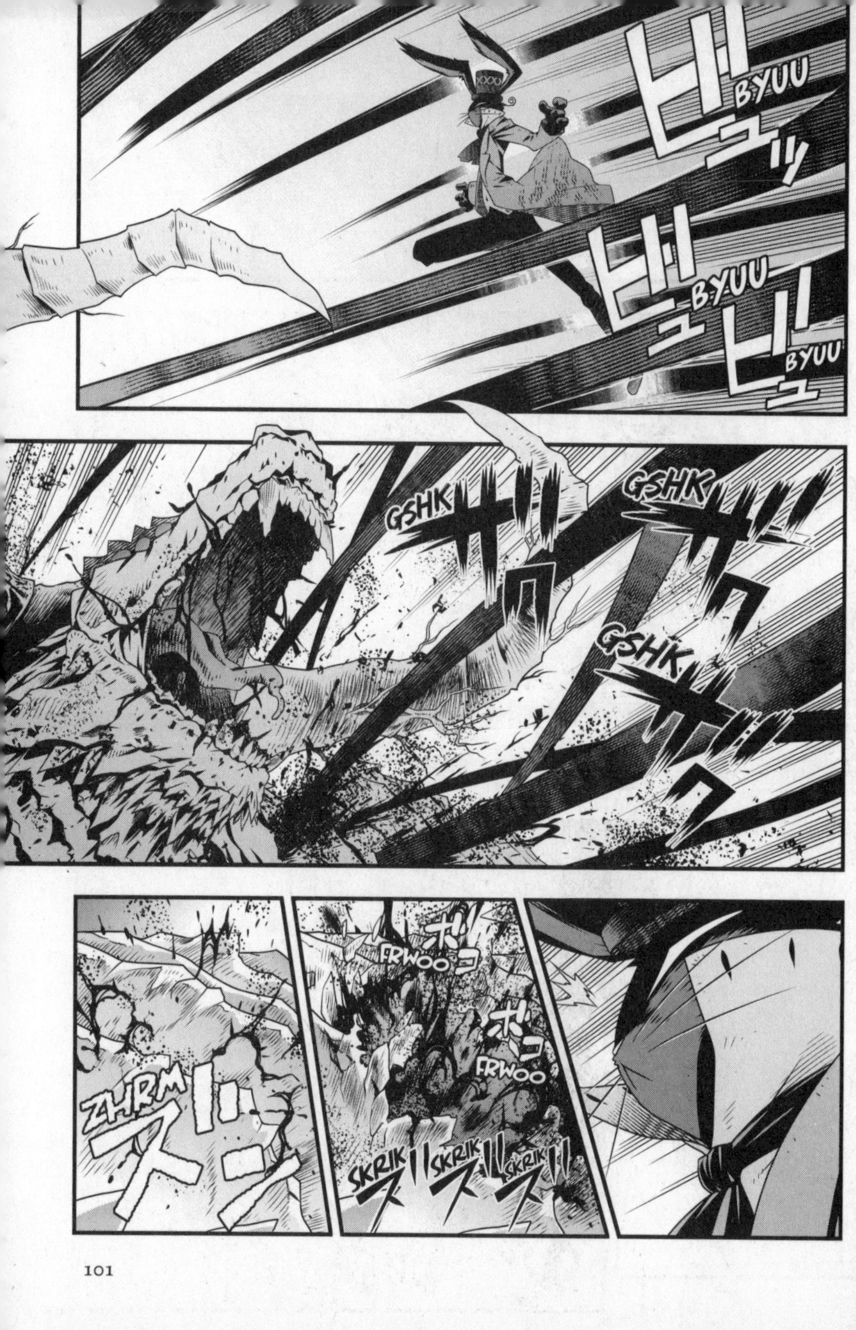
ビュッ
BYUU
ビュ
BYUU
ビュ
BYUU
ザク
GSHK
ザク
GSHK
ザク
GSHK
ボコ
FRWOO
ボコ
FRWOO
ズ!!
SKRIK
ズ!!
SKRIK
ズ!!
SKRIK
ズー…
ZHRM

THIS WILL BE A LONG BATTLE!
GRAAARRRHHH!
THUD
HEED ME! WHETHER OR NOT YOUR COMRADE YET LIVES, TAKE HIM AND GET TO SAFETY! QUICKLY, NOW!
TUG

FLOP
BWOOM
FWAM

SHLK
SHLK
SIZZZZZ
HMM? SURELY THIS CAN'T BE...?

SNAP
SNAP
SNAP

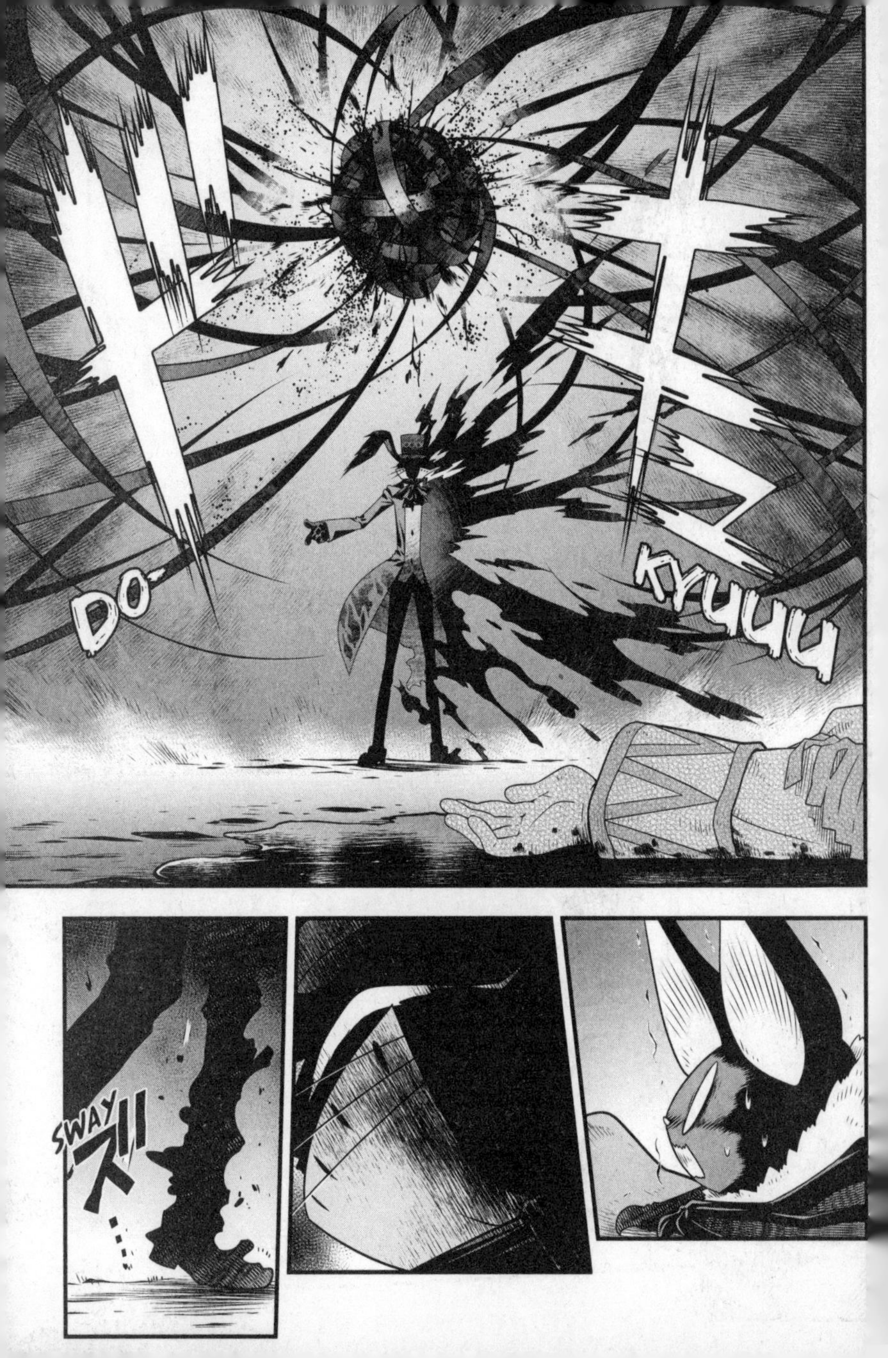
KYUUU
DO-
SWAY
ズ
...

ズッ…
SWAY
ズリ
SWAY
SWAY ズリ
ガクッ
THUD
SHAKE
SHAKE
SWAY
SWAY
SWAY
Driiip
TWITCH
TWITCH
TWITCH

......
......
WHAT IS THIS ...?
NOW...
COME, NOW.
WHAT IS THIS?
SOME SORT OF JOKE? HOW CAN THIS BE...?

NO, NO, THAT'S RIGHT. YOU WERE THE ONE WHO SAID IT-- **YOU** SPOKE THOSE WORDS.
YOU TOLD ME TO COME WITH YOU.
YOU.
IT WAS YOU.
WHAT ARE YOU DOING, THEN?
YOU SHOULD REJOICE. YES. THIS PLACE IS DARK, BUT WE SHALL GO TO THE LIGHT.
I WILL BE WITH YOU. NO NEED TO WORRY. I WILL ALWAYS BE WITH YOU. JUST OPEN YOUR EYES.
WHAT ARE YOU DOING? COME, WE ARE GOING ON A JOURNEY. A JOURNEY, I SAY. OPEN YOUR EYES.
PLEASE.
I WILL GIVE YOU ANYTHING, **ANYTHING** YOUR HEART DESIRES, SO--
"THERE'S NOTHING I WANT."

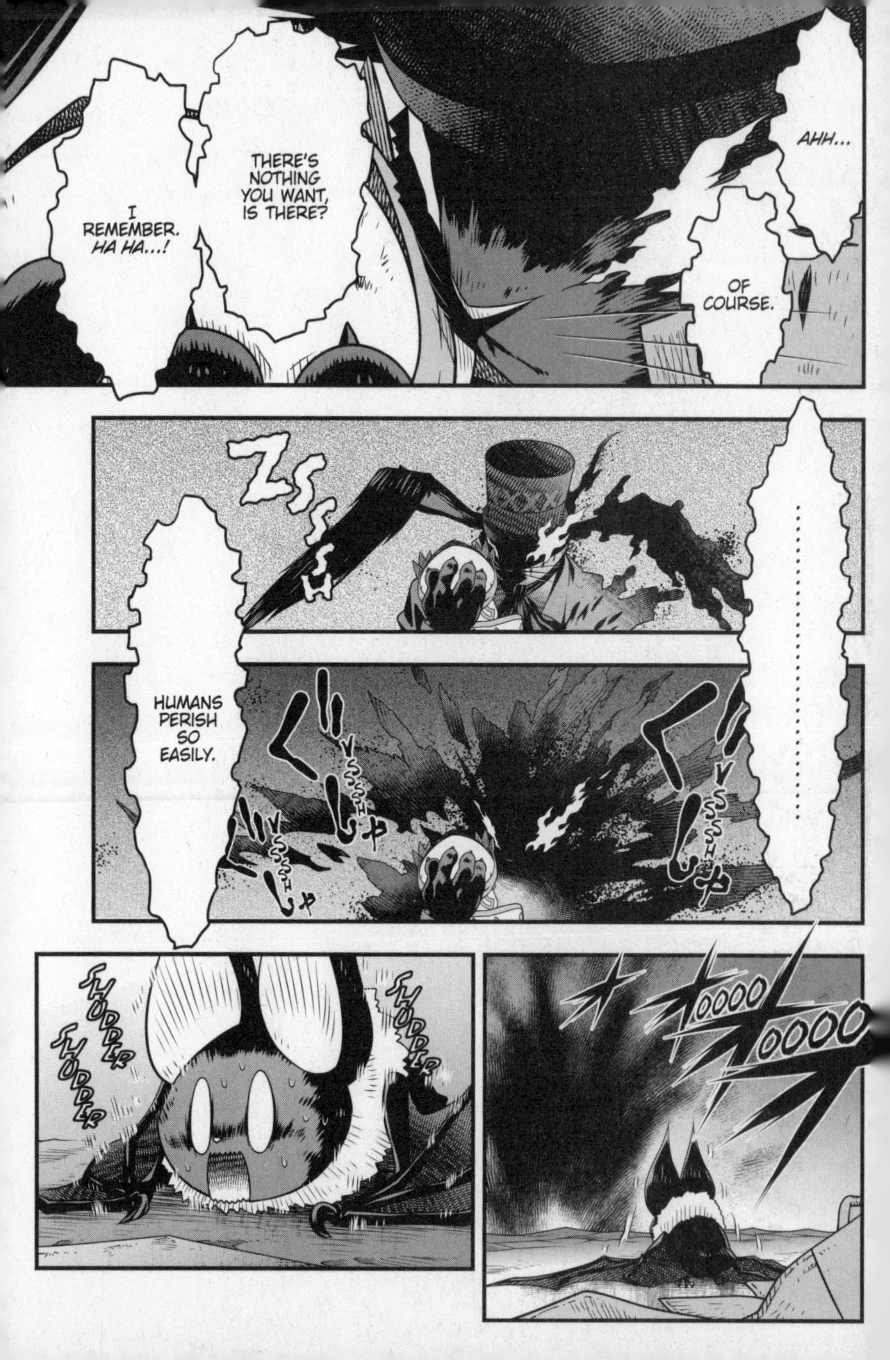
AHH...
OF COURSE.
THERE'S NOTHING YOU WANT, IS THERE?
I REMEMBER. HA HA...!
ZSSSH
......
HUMANS PERISH SO EASILY.
VSSSH
VSSSH
VSSSH
HOOOO
HOOOO
SHUDDER
SHUDDER SHUDDER

GWOOOOH
THWD
THWD
THWD
THWD
THWD
THWD
THWD

THWD
THWD
THWD
THWD
THWD
THWD
THWD
......
......!!
......
......

CRACK
CRACKLE
CRACK
"You must not hurt or kill humans."
HYOOM

SUCH A GOOD CHILD.

PERHAPS THE INVESTIGATOR WISHED TO KILL THE DRAGON. PERHAPS HE ALSO DESCENDED INTO MADNESS AS HE DIED. NO ONE WILL EVER BE CERTAIN WHY HE CURSED HIS OWN CORPSE.

LIKE FALLING FLOWER PETALS, THE YOUNG GIRL DIED PARTWAY THROUGH HER JOURNEY.
AND SO THE STORY ENDED.

Mythical Beast Investigator

FUUU...
HE WAS SEALED AWAY FOR A VERY, VERY LONG TIME.
FUUUU

[Chapter 10]
A Summer Night's Dream

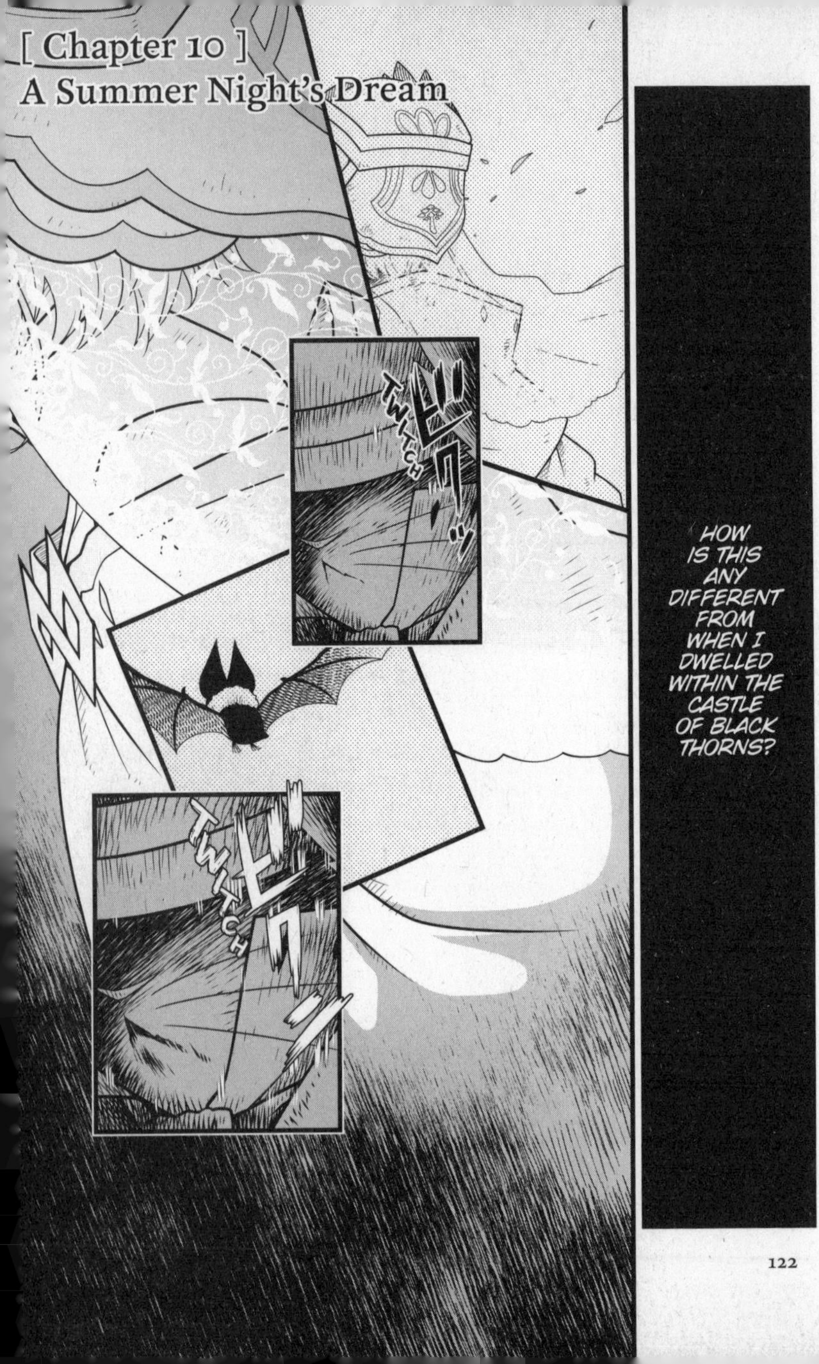

AHH. I REMEMBER YOU SAYING THAT TO ME.
"AFTER THAT, GO WHEREVER YOU PLEASE... BUT PROMISE ME THAT YOU'LL TAKE TROW WITH YOU. THAT WAY NEITHER OF YOU WILL BE LONELY."
HOWEVER, THE LITTLE BRAT IS NO LONGER HERE.

"INSTEAD OF STAYING IN SUCH A DREADFULLY LONELY PLACE...
"I THINK YOU SHOULD COME WITH ME."

I CALLED YOU A POISONOUS INSECT OVER AND OVER AGAIN. NEVER ONCE DID I CALL YOU A FLOWER.
I NEVER EVEN TOLD YOU MY NAME.

YOU...
YOU ARE...
WONDER-FUL! I SUCCEEDED!

HELLO! I AM FERRY EACHNA.
HOW ARE YOU FEELING?
FERRY... EACHNA.
SHE...
SHE HAD A DIFFERENT NAME.
YOU.
YOU LOOK JUST LIKE HER, YET YOU ARE A DIFFERENT HUMAN?
REGARDLESS-- NO. WHY DID THE SEAL...
THIS BOOK TOLD ME HOW TO RELEASE YOU.
THAT BOOK?

YOU SEE...
FWP...
IF, DURING HIS TRAVELS, THE KING OF DARKNESS WERE EVER SEALED AWAY...
THE INSTRUCTIONS FOR USING THE POWER OF YOUR SHADOW TO RELEASE YOU COULD BE FOUND IN THE "KING OF DARKNESS" SECTION.
BUT THE ME WHO WAS WITH YOU...
SHE WAS A DIFFERENT EACHNA.
SHE DIDN'T HAVE ANY REASON TO THINK SHE'D DIE SO ABRUPTLY.
SHE HADN'T FINISHED ALL OF THE CALCULATIONS TO BREAK THE SEAL.
IT TOOK ME A LONG TIME TO FIGURE IT OUT. I'M VERY SORRY.
"THE ME WHO WAS WITH YOU"?
"A DIFFERENT EACHNA"?

ARE YOU...
PER-HAPS...
NOT HUMAN, THEN?
NO, I AM HUMAN.
HOW-EVER...
I MAY NOT *EXACTLY* FIT THE STANDARD DEFINITION OF THE TERM.
A LONG, LONG TIME AGO...
THERE WAS A CERTAIN DAUGHTER OF A MYTHICAL BEAST INVESTIGATOR.

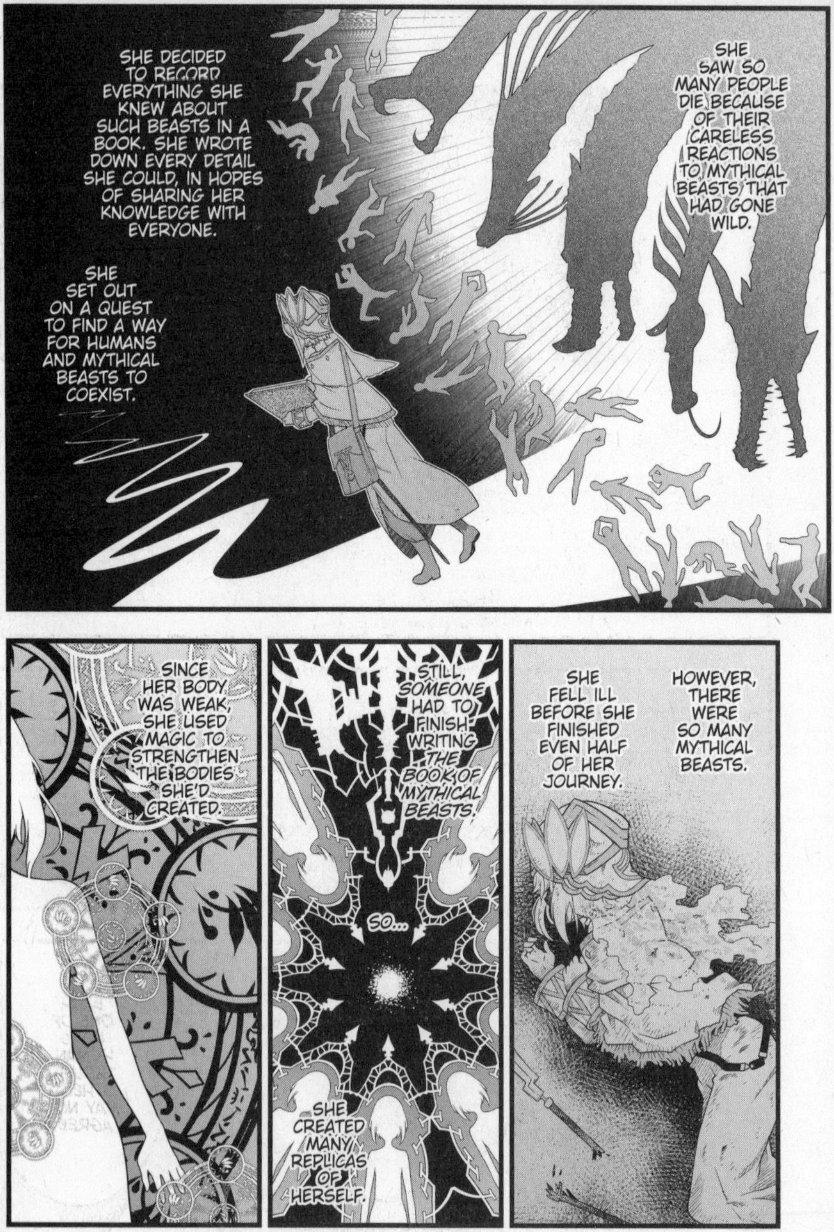
SHE SAW SO MANY PEOPLE DIE BECAUSE OF THEIR CARELESS REACTIONS TO MYTHICAL BEASTS THAT HAD GONE WILD.
SHE DECIDED TO RECORD EVERYTHING SHE KNEW ABOUT SUCH BEASTS IN A BOOK. SHE WROTE DOWN EVERY DETAIL SHE COULD, IN HOPES OF SHARING HER KNOWLEDGE WITH EVERYONE.
SHE SET OUT ON A QUEST TO FIND A WAY FOR HUMANS AND MYTHICAL BEASTS TO COEXIST.
HOWEVER, THERE WERE SO MANY MYTHICAL BEASTS.
SHE FELL ILL BEFORE SHE FINISHED EVEN HALF OF HER JOURNEY.
STILL, SOMEONE HAD TO FINISH WRITING *THE BOOK OF MYTHICAL BEASTS.*
SO...
SHE CREATED MANY REPLICAS OF HERSELF.
SINCE HER BODY WAS WEAK, SHE USED MAGIC TO STRENGTHEN THE BODIES SHE'D CREATED.

SHE CAST A CURSE ON HERSELF SO THAT IF SHE DIED, HER SOUL WOULD AWAKEN IN ONE OF THOSE BODIES.
A CURSE?
AT ONE TIME, IN THE PROCESS OF VERIFYING THE EXISTENCE OF FAE, A SORCERER DEVISED A METHOD TO CAPTURE A SOUL.
THE FIRST **"ME"** COMBINED THAT METHOD AND THE HOMUNCULUS'S ABILITIES ONCE SHE'D LEARNED TO REPLICATE HER PHYSICAL BODY.
SHE ALSO DISCOVERED A WAY TO GAIN ETERNAL LIFE, BUT...
SHE REJECTED THE IDEA OF USING IT, SINCE IT REQUIRED SACRIFICING OTHERS.
ALL OF THAT IS WHY, IF I DIE...
A *NEW* ME WILL AWAKEN. MY MEMORIES WILL NOT BE TRANSFERRED, BUT THE BODY AND SOUL WILL BE THE SAME.
EACH ONE OF US IS HUMAN, THOUGH OTHERS MAY NOT AGREE.
BUT *I* BELIEVE THAT I AM, AND I HAVE CHOSEN TO REMAIN HUMAN. AND AS A HUMAN, I'VE DECIDED WHAT I MUST DO.

AFTER ALL, IF I WERE NEITHER HUMAN NOR MYTHICAL BEAST...
HOW COULD I CLAIM TO BE CREATING A BETTER WORLD FOR THEM?
IT MAY ALL BE A LITTLE STRANGE, BUT...
THAT IS MY CONCLU-SION.
I HAVE CHOSEN MY DUTY.
ALL LIVING CREATURES CAN WALK THEIR OWN PATH, REGARDLESS OF WHAT THEIR PARENTS WANT FOR THEM.
I CHOOSE TO CONTINUE LIVING THIS WAY BECAUSE I LOVE BOTH HUMANS AND MYTHICAL BEASTS.
AND COMPLETING *THE BOOK OF MYTHICAL BEASTS* IS...
MY--OUR--WISH.

I LEARNED ABOUT THE KING OF DARKNESS BY READING THIS BOOK.
TWO OF MY PREVIOUS SELVES FOUND OUT ABOUT YOU THE EXACT SAME WAY.
WE ALL WANTED TO SAVE YOU, KNOWING YOU WERE SEALED AWAY.
THE ONE WHO TRAVELED WITH YOU HOPED THAT AFTER HER DEATH...
YOU COULD LIVE FREELY IN THIS BEAUTIFUL WORLD.
BUT THAT'S NOT WHAT HAPPENED.
BEFORE ANY OF US COULD EVEN ENTER THIS ROOM, WE HAD TO WAIT UNTIL THE HIGHER-UPS AMONG THE MYTHICAL BEAST INVESTIGATORS HAD ALL BEEN REPLACED, AND UNTIL EVERYONE HAD FORGOTTEN ABOUT THIS SEAL.
AFTER THAT, REMOVING THE SEAL TOOK A LONG TIME, TOO.
BUT HERE WE ARE AT LAST. I'M SO GLAD!

IT REPEATS...
SWAY
IT IS REPEATING NOW.
SWAY
SWAY
TH-THUMP...
WOULD YOU LIKE TO ACCOMPANY ME?
WHY...?
WHY WHAT?
WHY MUST I GO WITH YOU?

BECAUSE ALONE, WE'RE BOTH LONELY.
IS THAT WHY YOU RELEASED ME?
IN ORDER TO DRAG ME DOWN WITH YOU ONCE AGAIN?
SUCH SELFISHNESS!
NO, THAT'S NOT IT AT ALL! I DON'T WANT TO LEAVE YOU ALONE!
THE BOOK SAYS THAT YOU ARE TREMENDOUSLY KIND.
I JUST DIDN'T WANT SOMEONE SO KIND TO LIVE ALL ALONE, TRAPPED IN THE DARKNESS!

I KEPT THINKING ABOUT HOW LONELY YOU MUST HAVE BEEN, LOCKED AWAY IN A PLACE LIKE THIS.
YOU DON'T HAVE TO COME WITH ME.
THAT'S WHY I... THAT'S WHY *WE* CAME TO GET YOU.
I SIMPLY DIDN'T WANT YOU TO STAY IN SUCH A LONELY PLACE. THAT'S ALL.
MY ONLY WISH IS FOR YOU TO LOVE THIS WORLD THAT YOU LIVE IN.

I HOPE THAT THE KING OF DARKNESS, WHO WAS CREATED TO DESTROY THIS WORLD...
WILL LIVE ALONGSIDE ALL THE BEAUTIFUL THINGS HERE.

BUT IT WOULD CERTAINLY MAKE ME HAPPY IF YOU DID COME ALONG WITH ME.
AH. THAT'S RIGHT.
BACK THEN, WHEN YOU ASKED ME TO COME WITH YOU...
YOU MUST HAVE BEEN LONELY AS WELL.
I...
I AM NO LONGER THE KING OF DARKNESS.

MY NAME IS KUSHUNA TURATEIN.
I SHALL GO WITH YOU...
MY FLOWER AMONG THE POISONOUS INSECTS.

AND NOW, TODAY.
PEEK
KUSHUNA?
WHAT IS IT?
OH, NOTHING. IT JUST SEEMED ODD...
WHAT DOES?

IT'S UNUSUAL FOR YOU TO STAY IN YOUR PHYSICAL FORM AND SLEEP, THAT'S ALL.
I SUPPOSE SO.
PERHAPS IT WILL SNOW TOMORROW.
SUMMER IS NEARING ITS END, BUT NOT THAT QUICKLY, SURELY?
PERHAPS IT WILL RAIN FLOWERS TOMORROW.
HA HA!
THAT SOUNDS WONDERFUL.
IT WOULD SUIT MY FLOWER BEAUTIFULLY.
HISSS
I LOVE FLOWERS AS WELL.
IT IS SAID THAT THE SOUL INSIDE THE HOMUNCULUS...
RECORDS INFORMATION AND MEMORIES WITHIN ITS BONES. MY FLOWER RECOVERED HIM AND TRIED TO REVIVE HIM, BUT IT WAS UNSUCCESSFUL.
FLICK
THEREFORE, I ADDED A BIT OF MY OWN MAGIC TO THE TASK.
WE COULD NOT RECOVER HIS MEMORIES.
HE IS NOT PRECISELY AS HE WAS, BUT I AM HAPPY TO SEE HIM AGAIN.

SNAP
SO, MY FLOWER. WHAT ARE OUR PLANS FOR TOMORROW?
SNAP
I WAS THINKING OF HEADING EAST OF THE FOREST.
I SEE. AND AFTER THAT?
I DO NOT KNOW.
IF THERE ARE ANY PROBLEMS BETWEEN HUMANS AND MYTHICAL BEASTS, WE WILL SOLVE THEM.
IF WE FIND ANY NEW MYTHICAL BEASTS, I WILL RECORD THEM IN THE BOOK.

WHAT THEY LOVE, WHAT THEY YEARN FOR...
WHAT THEY HATE, AND WHERE THEY WANT TO LIVE...
SO THAT THE LACK OF KNOWLEDGE WILL NOT CAUSE GRIEF BETWEEN HUMANS AND MYTHICAL BEASTS.

IN ORDER FOR THEM TO LIVE IN HARMONY, I WILL REPEAT THE CYCLE AS MANY TIMES AS IT TAKES.
AS YOU WISH, MY FLOWER AMONG INSECTS.
IF THAT IS WHAT YOU WISH FOR, INSTEAD OF OBTAINING ALL THIS WORLD HOLDS...
I WILL COME WITH YOU, AT LEAST UNTIL YOUR WISH IS GRANTED.
TO BEGIN WITH, THERE IS NOWHERE ELSE I WANT TO BE.

CROCKLE
CROCKLE
SHFF
FWOO...

Mythical Beast Investigator

[Final Chapter] The Girl of White, the King of Darkness, and the Homunculus

ZA-ZAA
ZA-ZAA
EEEEE!
EEEEEE!

STROKE
すりすり
GOOD.
EVERYTHING IS NORMAL.
THE DATA ON A HOMUNCULUS'S SOUL IS CARVED INTO THEIR BONES, BUT...
IT'S IMPORTANT TO GIVE THEM REGULAR PHYSICAL CHECKUPS TOO.

MOST CERTAINLY.
CHIRP CHIRP CHIRP...
BY THE WAY...
I AM MOST CERTAINLY NOT RESPONDING HALFHEARTEDLY OUT OF JEALOUSY THAT HE IS BEING PETTED, UNDERSTAND?
THAT IS VERY TRUE.

I'M SORRY, KUSHUNA. DID YOU SAY SOMETHING?
TURN
I...
SAID...
NOTHING!
BONE, HMM?
ALL THOSE MANY, MANY YEARS AGO...

AFTER THE GIRL IN WHITE DIED...
TROW'S BONES WERE LEFT BEHIND IN THE LAND OF THE ANCIENT DRAGON.
THE SKELETON OF SUCH A BRAVE HERO, ABANDONED IN SUCH A MISERABLE STATE.
THE PAIR EVENTUALLY RECOVERED HIS REMAINS AND REVIVED HIM.

THEY ARE THE SAME, YET THEY ARE NOT.
I AM QUITE CERTAIN THERE CAN BE NOTHING MORE DEAR.

I THINK I NEED TO FURTHER EXAMINE HIM.
KUSHUNA...
WILL YOU TELL ME A STORY?
A STORY?
HMM. I AM NO MINSTREL.
I AM NOT A GIFTED STORY-TELLER, MY FLOWER.

OH?
YOUR VOICE IS VERY SOOTHING, AND YOU SPEAK SO SMOOTHLY.
THERE IS NO ONE ELSE I'D RATHER HEAR A STORY FROM.
///
PERK
COUGH
THIS IS A STORY FROM LONG, LONG AGO.
THERE WAS A LONELY KING OF DARKNESS, HOLED UP IN HIS PALACE.

ZA-
ZAAA

IT IS THE TALE OF HOW THAT LONELY KING MET A CERTAIN YOUNG GIRL.

CLAP
ALL RIGHT!
WE'RE DONE, TROW. THERE WERE NO ABNORMALITIES. GOOD WORK!
シャキーン
SHA-KIIING

FLAP
FLAP
FLAP
FLAP
FLAP
FLAP
THANK YOU, KUSHUNA.
HEARING YOUR STORY MADE ME VERY HAPPY.
YES.
IF MY FLOWER IS SATISFIED, IT WAS WORTH TELL...
TONK
ぎゅむ
SQUISH
HEY, LITTLE BRAT!
MY HAT IS *NOT* FOR LANDING ON!
HEY!

SO, KUSHUNA...
WHAT HAPPENED TO THE KING OF DARKNESS AND THE GIRL IN WHITE?
IS IT NOT OBVIOUS?
ALL FAIRY TALES END IN THE SAME WAY, DO THEY NOT?

"AND SO, THE TWO OF THEM CONTINUED THEIR JOURNEY...
"AND LIVED HAPPILY EVER AFTER."

FLAP FLAP FLAP
SLAP
ペチッ
SLAP
ペチッ
......!

WELL, THEN.
LET US BE ON OUR WAY, MY FLOWER.
SHUP
YES!

LET'S GO TOGETHER!

THIS IS THE STORY ABOUT HOW THAT LONELY KING OF DARKNESS MET A CERTAIN GIRL OVER AND OVER AGAIN.

Fin

Mythical Beast Investigator

あとがき Afterword

It was while I was mired deep in some personal problems that I was invited to adapt *Mythical Beast Investigator* into a manga. The world Ayasato-sensei created is beautiful and kind, yet very tough. The realism of it gave me hope even after I finished reading it, and lack's illustrations opened my eyes to a beautifully lush world. I truly believe that *Mythical Beast Investigator* is amazing.

My time working on this project was brief, but it was a joyful time. I gained a lot from it, and I would like other people to share in that feeling.

As a fan, I hope to continue reading the *Mythical Beast Investigator* novels and support the author. I'd like to thank Ayasato-sensei, lack, my readers, and the publisher!!

星野倖一郎
Koichiro Hoshino

Mythical Beast Investigator